YOUR BRAIN

The Engine to Your Body

Your Brain

The Engine to Your Body

Kids Edition

ISBN- 9798684213632

The author disclaims responsibility for adverse effects or consequences from the misapplication or injudicious use of the information contained in this book. Mention of resources and associations does not imply an endorsement.

Illustrations by Puneet Kumar

YOUR BRAIN

The Engine to Your Body

Kids Edition

By Tracy Markley

Hello!

My name is Tracy.

I want to help you learn about your brain.

Your body relies on your brain to move and function.

Your brain is the engine to your body,
so you must treat it nicely and keep it healthy.

You were born with about
100 billion neurons in your brain.

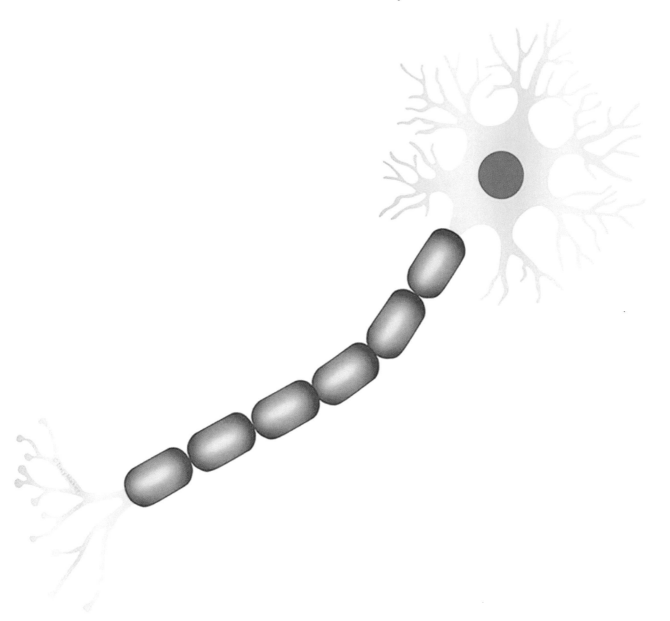

This is a neuron.

A neuron is also known as a cell.
These cells communicate with the whole body.

Neurons send messages through your body to help you walk, jump, speak, raise your hands, run, skip, blink your eyes, see, hear, and all movements in your body.

Neurons send their messages through transmitters that are called "dopamine". One neuron throws out dopamine as another neuron catches the dopamine.

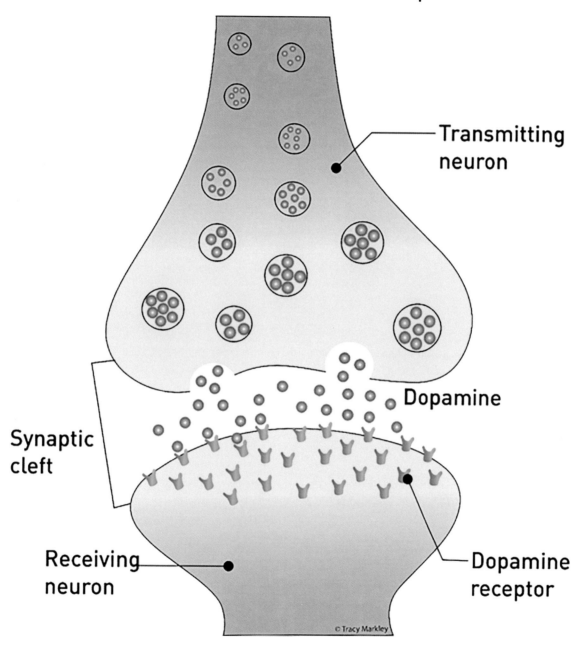

In this picture the pink balls are the dopamine.

This is all happening in the space between the two neurons. This space is called the synaptic cleft.

The neurons in your brain stay healthier when you eat healthy food, drink plenty of water and exercise.

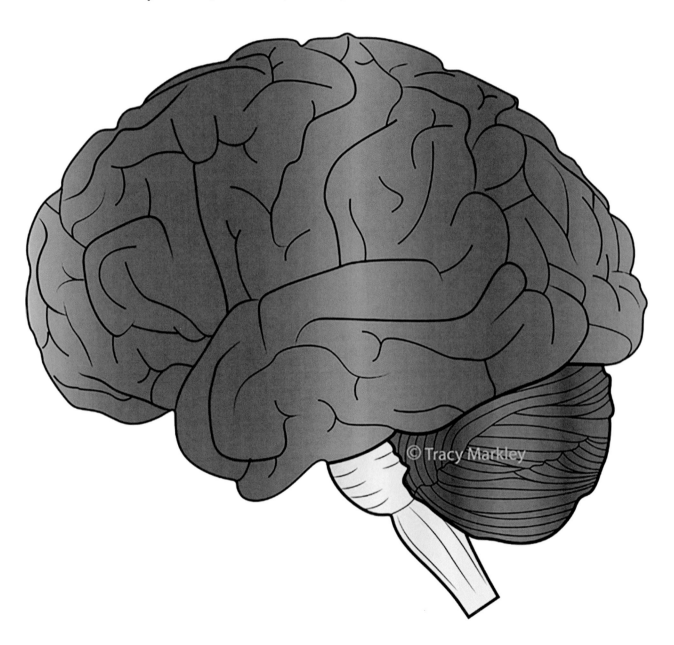

A healthy brain helps you to have a healthy body.

Your brain is made up of about 80% water.
It needs water to be healthy and to perform its best job.

Drinking plenty of water keeps
your brain hydrated and healthy.

This helps you to think more clearly and feel better.

Be sure to drink enough water every day.

In fact, it is good for you to drink a full glass of water when you wake up in the morning. This helps hydrate your brain after going hours without drinking any water as you sleep at night.

Your brain needs to be fed healthy foods too.
Eat more fruits and vegetables instead of junk food.

Your brain needs the vitamins and minerals
that healthy foods naturally supply.

It is fun to plant your own garden and watch it grow too.

Eating fruits and vegetables fresh from the garden is an extra healthy thing to do.

Laughter can increase endorphins. Endorphins make you feel good and keep you in a good mood.

Laughter can also increase the oxygen to your brain.

Your brain requires oxygen to function.

So having a good laugh and giggles with your family and friends are healthy things to do. Laughing is fun!

Some people have hearing loss and need to wear hearing aids. I wear hearing aids.

When we do not hear well, it can make our brains extra tired. Tell your parents if you think you may be having trouble hearing in school.

Hearing aids will help you hear
your teachers and friends more clearly.

You can still play and have fun like other kids
even if you wear hearing aids.

You require daily exercise to have a healthy body and brain. So play and have fun.

Exercise helps the brain to be healthy and maintain the healthy functions needed for everyday activities.

Remember, your brain is the engine to your body as an engine is to a car. The engine in a car must be taken care of so the car can drive and last a long time.

How you feed and hydrate your brain today will affect how it can work at its best tomorrow and in the future days and years to come.

As you age your brain ages with you. The better you take care of it every day, the stronger it will be as you grow.

Exercising, staying hydrated, and eating healthy foods will make you a stronger teenager and a stronger adult. It will help you focus, learn, and get better grades in high school and college.

Learning new things is healthy for brain cell activity. Learning helps keep the neurons in your brain strong.

Even when you become an adult, learning new things will help your brain stay strong. You should learn new things for fun but also to keep your brain working properly.

Remember to be kind.

Kindness makes people feel good.

Feeling good is healthy for your brain.

So be kind to yourself and be kind to others too.

It can help others feel good and help them
to have healthy brains as well!

YOU ARE NICE!

GREAT JOB!

YOU ARE SMART!

THANK YOU!

YOU ARE UNIQUE!

YOU ARE SPECIAL!

About the Author

Tracy Markley is a fitness specialist and author. She has been in the health and fitness industry for over twenty years. Her clientele range between the ages of 6 to 105 years old. Her previous books have been on brain care, neuroplasticity, stroke recovery, spine anatomy, core strength and fall prevention. She is an educator and has received awards for her work. She is also the host of *The Health and Fitness Show with Tracy* at KXCR radio on the Oregon Coast. Her other books can be found at her website and at www.amazon.com/author/tracymarkley She can be reached at www.tracymarkley.com

Made in the USA
Middletown, DE
23 August 2024